M000097920

this book

BELONGS TO

---

oh Yes WE DiD™

Made in the USA
Columbia, SC
25 November 2020

25536996R00065